ONLY BLEED

From Sorrow to Strength

By

Vernon D. Lloyd
with
Geneva Baker Cotton

Only Mothers Bleed
From Sorrow to Strength

By

Vernon D. Lloyd
w/Geneva Baker Cotton

Published by
Grown Folks Productions

In Memory, of

Dr. Doris V. Bright

Dedication

Stephanie Harris-Hollowell
Julia Spencer
Charlotte Robinson
Paulicia Conley
Carla King

And

Kylen Guinn
4/12/97 – 10/9/16

Table of Contents

Acknowledgments

When a mother goes into the delivery room there are very few that are allowed in there. In most cases, there is the doctor plus one or two nurses along with up to two persons for the one giving birth. However, along the way there are several people who help to make the journey more informed, stronger, and enjoyable. They do so by many ways that impact the lives of the mother, father and the child. We should always be grateful for them.

As it is in pregnancy, so it is in writing. Many have helped us as we have worked to produce this work. Some were not in the delivery room but they were there to help us bring things through sharing insights, experiences, encouragement, ears, eyes and time that cannot be measured.

Special thanks to Dr. Michelle Harris who has been relentless in her efforts to touch hurting women with this message and bring great awareness to it through hands on ministry, her blog-talk radio show, Vindicated Magazine and the pulpits she ministers in throughout the country. She is also in the process of a major documentary that gives great awareness and assistance in dealing with mothers who have suffered the tragedies of senseless street murder, gang violence, domestic violence police brutality and suicide. Her drive is vital to this movement and organization.

Special thanks to Bishop Clarence Haddon and Prophetess Joyce Haddon for their continued support in ministering to wounded and hurting mothers, to Ms. Jamilah Halverson for your moral and financial support of the Only Mothers Bleed Initiative, to Mr. Thom Cotton for being a supporter is spirit and for the sacrifice of time that makes what we do possible. Special thanks also to Mrs. Lillie Parks- Cox for valuable insight and time that opened new venues of understanding. We are grateful for collaborative our partner Males to Men of Atlanta, Georgia for your assistance in our media projects and community outreach. We give thanks to the Detroit, MI and Chicago, IL. Areas that have assisted us in many ways to make this movement and this project a reality. Your continuing support is invaluable to all that we do and all that we will be able to do. Finally, we thank you, the reader of this book for your support. You help us express what needs to be shared and empower us to say more of it. God bless you all for all that you bless us with.

Preface

Kylen Guinn
4/12/97 – 10/9/16

Preface

One beautiful Spring day in 1997 the announcement went forth that a baby boy had arrived. This announcement culminated a long journey of one who brought joy to the life of his mother. As she viewed and held him she knew that she held someone special. There was real purpose in his life. Kylen Guinn came into the world with the promise of a bright future and with a spirit that would reign throughout his life.

He was raised, along with his brother, by a mother who was steeped in her faith and gave him to God at an early age. They were the lights of her life and forces that compelled her to seek the best for them. She knew that keeping them in the hands of God was the best place to keep him and she honored that giving by placing them before great mentors and examples who could help shape his ideas of what it meant to live a true Christian life.

Kylen was kind and impressionable. He was inquisitive and sensitive. He had a heart that felt for other people and felt other people. His arms reached out and where he could not reach he tried to get others to do so. Two of his favorite people were Bishop Clarence Haddon and Prophetess Joyce Haddon. Around the church, he watched them and took what they said and did to heart while implementing it in the dimensions in which he lived. He was inquisitive and active. He found a regular place around them and made certain there was no lacking their attention. He learned well and sought to live as he had observed their lifestyle. He mimicked it at home, at school and in the community. He was a unique child.

However, life happens and as every child experiences, the pressures of growing up intensified and Kylen faced them too. The adjustment from the disciplines of home to trying to do things in a manner unfamiliar to him caused some problems and got him involved in some situations that proved tragic for him. His steps strayed from the path that had been mapped for him but he took that same self with him. He did not fit where he sought to frequent. His life ran into contradiction. He left home for church on October 9, 2016 with the intent to invest in his turnaround. On the way, he encountered one detour led him to an unfortunate and tragic end.

Kylen was gunned down. He suffered multiple gunshot wounds and was left in the street. What was the cause for it? Nothing! A light for his mother Stephanie Harris-Hollowell, went out. Her heart bled. One who held such hope now was gone too soon. Sorrow was the first emotion but she determined that it would not be her last state.

She determined that the blood shed by her son would not dry and be forgotten but would serve as the seed to bring hope and life to others. She determined to move from sorrow to strength and do all that she could to insure there was help and hope for mothers who have suffered loss as she has. She has become a crusader to work to reduce the number of deaths experienced due to gang violence, domestic violence, senseless murders in communities, suicide and other avoidable loss of life. Kylen is her inspiration. He died but he is not done.

Kylen is our inspiration along with thousands who have suffered as he has. The mothers whose hearts have suffered through these losses are the primary targets of our efforts. Thomas Aquinas once said, "The blood of the martyrs is the seed of the church." We adopt this saying in spirit believing that all life is precious and no drop of blood goes wasted and that every life tragically taken is the seed for growing a community that will not tolerate or facilitate violence. We believe that the blood of victims like Kylen is the seed for the Only Mothers Bleed Movement. We ask you to join us as we seek to lead others from Sorrow to Strength.

Introduction

"She shall be called Eve for she shall be the mother of all living" Life is a blood transaction. It is one man and one woman exchanging life in each other. It is humanity participating with Divinity in the extension and continuing expression of people. It is a true privilege to do so.

The man gives and the woman grows or nurtures. The womb is the dressing room for the world. She is the one who bears the child and cares for it until it comes to full maturity and demands out. She bonds with it like no one else can and before it is ever born she has a relationship unlike one that anyone else could. She talks to it. She feds it. Here care of herself is that of her child. This result of a dynamic interaction of ovum and sperm in the closed quarters of a fallopian tube has generated a source of great joy and sometimes a great discomfort that she does not mind bearing. A mother loves her children and there is nothing that she will not do even to the point of death for them.

It is said that when a child is growing that it is always pulling on heartstrings but when they are grown they are on their heart strings. There is never a severing. There is a feeling that never ceases to be whether in life or in death.

In this book, you shall experience instruction, insight, inspiration and engagement. It presents different scenarios that permit you to be a part of the understanding the lives of women who have suffered through a variety of loss and ultimately gone from sorrow to strength. You will go through it with them and walk away with better understanding and determination to cease the violence.

The drama in loss is tremendous particularly when it happens suddenly and right under your nose. We seek to bring this out here. It is never to be taken lightly or presumptively. It is traumatic and takes time to heal from and move on to wholeness. We must be careful in dealing with others who have suffered. It is a nurturing process that requires open minds, hearts and arms.

As you approach this book please do so with the understanding that it is not a book of poetry just flung together. It is a work brought expressed in poetry and verse (to simplify the message) that seeks to draw you into personal experiences. It seeks to make them real and to draw you into the mindset of those who are going through various challenges. We hope that you will take time to reflect on what you read and how you may respond. Use the pages at the end of each piece to engage yourself or interact with others in a group setting. Thank you for journeying with us. God bless you.

A Word Especially for You:

There is a low place that we go when tragedy strikes without notice and senselessly. It is a place that seeks a grip and does not release us easily therefore you must be willing to break through. You must be willing to take the situation and transform it. That is what it means to go from sorrow to strength.

In the Only Mothers Bleed Movement that is what we seek to help mothers to do who have experienced loss of children to violence and must cope with violence their children may be engaging in. The knock on the door or the phone call that announces that a child or loved one is dead is one of the most heart wrenching things that can happen. The place that it takes one is almost as harsh as the death. We seek to take that life-giving energy in every mother and pass it on after the tragedy. There shall never be shed a drop of blood that is wasted. Mothers bleed to bear and to birth a child. They bleed in raising that child and are willing to bleed, continue to give life, for that child.

Only Mothers Bleed is a Ministry, with a Message and Mission designed to lay the foundation for a movement to empower hurting women, to provide help, healing, wholeness and honor. It is dedicated to the reduction of senseless murders, gang violence, suicide, police brutality and domestic abuse. Its vision is broad but its venues provide it the opportunity to reach it with participation from people like you. For more information please email us at **OnlyMothersBleed@gmail.com** or visit our Facebook page Only Mothers Bleed.

Geneva Baker-Cotton

ONLY MOTHERS BLEED

The deepest levels of love are not found in the hands, the arms, the eyes and words of a mother but in the heart, that beats and bleeds for the child conceived in and that comes forth from her ~ Vern

ONLY MOTHERS BLEED

And God said "Let there be...
Until He
Me
And We
Then I heard...
BE...
Fruitful and multiply
Replenish the earth
I out of him
He into me
We
From I
And
The blood flows
I bleed...
Alone
Come to me
Enter and dwell
Share and cultivate
Place the good
And leave it to be
Stirred and situated
Come forth and into
I feed the seed
I release what meets
What is released then cage it
Feeding it
Caressing and containing
Kings and queens
Rulers on deposit
Geniuses and philosophers
World Changers
And the most subtle
Seemingly unengaged man

Who sneaks upon academia
And the most erudite
Explaining universal concepts
And eternal truths
 I bleed
I need not be cut
I am the pool
Civilization draws from
Every month I am possibility
Nile-like beyond Egypt
Fertile Crescent
Rising and falling
I am prepared
Seeking what may be
Cultivating and capturing
Prayed for
Fertile yet not always full
I wait
I am
Life giver
I am cradle and so necessary
That without me there is no other
To be called me
See without ground is seed
But not sown
Grown
Owned and replicated
Even if sown
If not held and fed
Made sick
Disproportionate when filled
Stretched
Marked and remembered
I bear then birth
Expelling what was minuscule
Thrusting into a world
Unknown
I bleed alone
Even when

In the blood of who I am
There is no life
Filling
Cramping at time
Bloated
Struggling for ¼ of a month
Irritated
I planned nothing here
This time but because I am who I am
I can be depended on
To Bleed
You see my drain
My pain
My "Oh no not again"
Popping Ibuprofen
Rocking like a baby
Cursing Eve and wondering
What it would have been like if…
Shunned during a time
I need sharing more
I Bleed…
Puberty then menopause
A long road
I bleed…
Bearing the inner and outer
I flow and carry
I birth and then the blood of me
Continues…
I feel
What is of my blood is of my being
My man flows
My children flow
My self flows…
Caught in an existential inescapable assignment
I bleed
Never ceasing
Comforting him
Birthing them
While I just…Bleed

I do not flaunt my blood
It is inside building
I release it privately
Like tears
And pain
Like sadness and disappointment
I bleed for my children living in breech
And for my man in his struggle
With dignity and impotence
Calling him forth
For he empowers me
And is me...I bleed
That he might come forth
As he did in his mother's womb
I call him
Come...dwell with me
Be of me
Remember
I am of your blood
Covering your very heart and breath
Come
No one can bear it like me
No one can help
It is heavy then lighter but IS
When nothing sown
Comes forth...
Feel my loneliness Adam
When you do not sow me
Forget me not for new streams
And fresher ones
I have given and...
Your legacy is in me
Your name is mine
I give life to you
I need your deposits
For long after childbearing years
Blood flows still to my heart
My mind
My body is full of vessels

Stimulated and delighted
Setting off things
That set you off
And fill me that you might know
The fullness of my filling
Stir my blood
Because a neglected heart bleeds
Inside OUT and then
When it overflows
It remains in places
Undesigned for it
Poisoning the vessel
That genuinely brings life
I bleed...
I cease the flow yet I do
Yet give birth
I have reproduced
What is yet flowing and will flow
I teach it
That it might continue
I bleed...
Remember that life is in me
Of me
I bleed
I am your life
Desiring your life
That we might feed what we seed
And grow forever

TALK ABOUT IT:

What I Read

What I Reflect on

What I Realize

How I Choose to Respond

How I can NOW reach out

FROM A GROWN WOMAN
TO A YOUNG LADY

Sit down baby and talk to me
Welcome to womanhood
Oh~ I know you've got the goods
The curves and parts that take the eyes
The legs, the breasts, the butt and thighs
And that's all good but you need to see
The new place you have among ladies
You are legal and on your way
To being a Grown lady one day BUT
Not quite yet

You see you have entered a new door
You are expected to know and to be more
You are fair game to many others on the field
Be careful of where you stop and to whom you yield
Learn before you leap and know before you go
Young lady be certain and take it slow
Talk to your mother and get some advice
She may not be all your flavor but you will get good spice

You may think this is not needed
But growness does not just happen it must be seeded
And womanhood from childhood/adolescence is a transition
You must work yourself into this new position
Hear me while hearing can be best communicated
Do not despise it not consider it over rated
For all you are and shall come to be
I have established and you shall inherit from me

Find your mentors and learn some valuable lessons
It will keep you from foolishness and distressing
If all your advice comes from those your age

You will make many mistakes upon this page…
Of life and so many times you will try to erase
Things that never should have held this space
Keep your friends and circle; you need them too
But to be successful you will need history before you

You cannot be grown on your mother's dime
So, before you demand sole independence keep this in mind
She can help you get what she has if you listen well
Do not lose her support coming under a spell
Of "doing your own thing because I am me"
Your mother is a grown woman and you will see
That when you go there she goes there too
And say woman to woman do what you must do

Get and education in class and in the way
Learn your lessons and let the wisdom stay
Train to become great and make a difference
Do not let these beginning lady days be ill spent
Enjoy the learning and consider it worth the time
Living and learning are like rhythm and rhyme
Get it all while it offers you unattached
Become who you will be and you can find the right match

See yourself from the inside out
Here well what I am talking about
Develop in the inner places and you can reveal
The person you are as authentic and so real
Other women can see you and appreciate you
Because your womanhood will be through and through
Not fake and pretentious for true women can see
When you are really who you claim to be

Develop your intellect, charm and true beauty
You are more than breasts, legs and booty
And if that is what you accentuate and often share
You will only be looked upon primarily there
You shall be a piece to be had but not to be cherished
After encounters you will see men and be embarrassed

You will be like a playground open all day
Where men love to come but only to play
Keep your legs closed to visitors and strangers around
Who will see you like lost money on the ground
The will claim you and spend you until you are gone
Then whistle, walk away and with you be done
Fund no brother by giving what you have been given
You are not responsible for his living
Work side by side in together in the field
Of growth and eventually there will be a yield

Pay your own bills and care for your own self
Keep all your valuables on a special self
Do not pimp yourself for a happy meal and done nails
Your cable bill paid and some exciting tail
You run yourself
You oversee you
Wait on some things
It is okay to do
Learn to be by yourself
Love yourself really good
Treat yourself in the manner
You desire that another would
Teach the world who you are
Teach it how to come face to face
And engage a woman like you
Full of beauty and grace

Build a good man
By being a good lady
Manhood not maleness
Sunshine not his shady
He need not be yours
But still make an impact
By doing with lady thing well
Living on your own track

And when you find the right one
Or should I say when he finds you

Make sure that not only to him
But also to yourself you are true
Give him who you are inside first and then
If he desires to love and know that person begin
To share your true self and see where it goes
Getting to know each other is a series of flows

Marry not for money, houses, fame or sex
If you do both you and he will soon holler "NEXT"
Marry for love and who you are and can be
Are you grasping this wisdom coming from me?
Stay in your lane and strengthen your hand
Be compromising but have an equal hand
Keep your home solid; keep mess out your house
Take care of your man first ~ he is YOUR SPOUSE
Keep folks out your business
Particularly your girls
Give them that special place
But this is your world
Keep your business out the street
And when others come to look
Do not let it be found live and in print
On Twitter, Instagram and Facebook

Get your stuff together
Keep your stuff tight
Own your dignity
Do what is right…
For you and keep taking strides
Of honor with loyalty and pride
Raise the standard and the banner too
Of what womanhood is as you do what you do

Trust a sister here and a sister there
Cut the negativity about mistrusting us and share
That thought all are not perfect and some are not good
We are ever evolving together in womanhood
Walk with me daughter and this I will teach
More than what I have shared in this speech

Slow down and do not seek what I have attained
It took me many years for all of this to gain

Let me share your dreams and help you grow
Let me help you go where you desire to go
Do not forget I have been where you are going
And you can excel if you pay attention to what I am showing
Watch where I stumbled and where I have fallen
And avoid those places when defeat comes calling
I am offering these things especially for you
So that you can better do what you need to do

Live with flavor
Live with SPICE
Be sanctified naughty
With the right one but nice
Be unique ~Be divine
Do who you are
Do not seek to be mine

Live young lady like a champion
Live until the first stages of lady are done
Then you can emerge on your very own
As a woman mature and fully grown
It is not about age but wisdom and experience
It is about knowledge and plain good sense
I am proud to look at you and see
The continuance of a grown woman legacy

So, let's rock it now and as we take our place
You and I are different sides of the face
Of a womanhood God ordained to His glory
We are vital pages in the womanhood story
Step up now and I will step further down the line
I shall prophesy you and you shall greater define
Who we are and what we do
Grow young lady until full grown…It is what you must do

TALK ABOUT IT:

What I Read

What I Reflect on

What I Realize

How I Choose to Respond

How I can NOW reach out

MOTHER'S PRAYER
(Cover Him)

Hello Lord
It's me again ~ Sadie
I know we just talked
And you sure can do some mighty fine talking
Of course, you been doing it longer than anyone
And I appreciate you hearing me
I was almost sleep when I heard the door close
And well...
My boy done gone out again
Yes ~ he's a good boy
He really is
We tried to raise him well
He got a few issues like ~

Well he drinks but you know that
He got a bad temper and cusses
Whew! That boy can cuss
But he is a good boy except them gals
A different one every week

I pray Lord that you keep him in those streets
Because he really is a good boy
Except he gambles his paycheck
And smoke them illegal marijuana weeds
He tells me they aint nothing but herbs
But I aint stupid

I tell him to smoke them in front of the police
And I will believe aint nothing to them
He really is a good boy
But he keeps getting in those fights
Raising hell all the time
And aint no God in that

He be stealing my money
But I steal it back
And he doesn't even know it
He driving with no license
And he got no money for bail or ticket
Lord protect my boy

He really is a good boy
Way down on the inside
It's just that stuff on top of that good boy
It is a heap of it
Smothering my baby down
Help him to come up

Because my boy really is a good boy
I gave him to you when he was born
And you said you'd take care of him
And I believe you sir
Because he should be dead the way he carries on
But he is walking around like a natural man

He's a good boy Lord
And I need you to help him be good tonight
Close the bars, doors and legs he would enter
They aint no good for him
And make him come home
And lie down and rest well

You have the power Lord
To make him behave
Take the tastes away
Dry up what he likes
Can you bring our baby back?
He got no darn business out there…
Ooops, sorry Lord
I did not mean to talk like that
I am going to sleep now Lord
I just wanted you to know he was gone

Since you are always up I am
going to lie down

Watch over my boy Lord
He really is good
You made him that way
He messed it up
But you are better at fixing
Than he is at messing up

I love you Lord
Have a good night
Tell that boy to use his key when he comes home
And be quiet
I reckon he will be here shortly
I know you have already got him pinned down
Is that the doorbell I hear?
It sure is…Lord that's my boy

 Hey son….

Home so soon…:
Everything must be well…
Closed huh?

TALK ABOUT IT:

What I Read

What I Reflect on

What I Realize

How I Choose to Respond

How I can NOW reach out

OWN YOUR OWN

(Growing Up Lessons)

So, you want your own
I understand that
Welcome to it
You have come of age
But you want it on your terms
ALONE
Using mine to get yours
Proclaiming inability
To what holds you
While funding to what you desire
Shunning my collaboration and consent
Where you certainly need support
Presuming it is okay
And living in a quiet defiance when it is not
I understand...
It is yours
Take it but mine cannot be yours
At the same time
To use as and when you please
That pollutes "OWN"
Release and receive
Cut the supply line
Accountability for my flow must be
Walk the path you cut
I shall cover my tracks from you
That you might make it on your OWN
Without referral or roots
Erased references
Cancelled history
Painful disconnect
You said yours was none of my business

Intrusive are my inquiries
And unnecessary my declarations
You are offended and I get it
I really do and honor where you are
I get it
For when you must be your OWN
You must own your OWN
Unmixed with any other
Pure OWN
OWN Responsibility
OWN Replenishing of pure Yours
OWN Purpose and place
No questions of you
No answers for you
Visitation rights
But not citizenships
Do not mix the two
Neither will I
I get it
Ask without presumption
Knowing that I respect your choice
Debt is paid
I owe you nothing
Neither do you owe me
Except for that which you borrow
To make your OWN
Free is a choice of mine
Not a privilege of yours
From this day, forth
Just one declaration
I love you...
On your own now child
Excuse me...On your beloved
OWN YOUR OWN

TALK ABOUT IT:

What I Read

What I Reflect on

What I Realize

How I Choose to Respond

How I can NOW reach out

There is a significant difference between being submissive to a person and being controlled by them. God is never abusive although He is in charge ~ Vern

SUBMISSION

She began
SUBMIT!
That is what we are told
Submit!
Let the man have control
Or better yet be the head
That is what is said... to US
Respect your man
I agree
I owe it to him
Like he owes it to me
I like a man in charge
I like that masculine cover
That secures and adores me
That is labeled my "for certain lover"
I think it is what God order
No, I know it to be true
So, if marriage is my thing
I do what I must do
At least that is how I feel
I need to be cared for
I need to be WITH someone
I do not just take a name
And then my life is done
I bring something to the table
That must be recognized
So, one cannot get it twisted
There will be no surprise
When I stand in my place
And present me as my own self
Not doing my man's expectation
I take me off the shelf
To show him first who I am
The type of rib that I present

Flexible without being compromising
I am unique without his consent
And if he sees that he will be blessed
He will be able to appreciate
That in living and serving in this life
He has more than HIM on his plate
That was and is my philosophy
And I made it strong and quite clear
But the one I connected with
Obviously did not take the time to quite hear
He started well
Yes, I was just right
No battle or fuss
No major fights
He expressed his take
On relationship and the make
He opened doors and walked with my hand
In his and I felt that he was a real man
His mother raised him
His daddy let him down
He was yet doing his thing
He would not let me down
Then he shared with me a beautiful ring
That made me holler and want to sing
He said he would love me till death do we part
He would give me his body, soul and heart
He would honor me and would understand when I say
To him I would love, honor and obey
Five years of heaven and then we went to hell
You will understand as this story I tell
He took over without any permission
To bring me, his wife, into total submission
Cursed one day and then threatened another
Jealousy raged and my person he smothered
His house not mine and his money too
Do what he wanted just because he wanted me to
Words got hard and he did not care
Where we were, he gave not a damn or a care
I became something less that a wife to him

I wanted out for life seemed grim
Then he said if I'd leave I would regret
The repercussion I certainly would get
He took my keys and regulated my time
My mama said hold on and toe the line
I expressed my concern but she said she knew best
He was just a man handling his own business
I ask if daddy had done the same to her
She said yes but challenging him created a stir
Besides, he paid the bills and worked all day
So, she let him say all that he wanted to say
It was how men were and would certainly be
So, she expects the same honor out of me
I said that I would hang on and do my best
But I need to get some things off my chest
No man would cause me to bow out in life
And own me like a slave yet be called his wife
I spoke to my man to make that perfectly clear
That brother looked at me and said "My dear
You know I love you and would not say
Anything to mislead you in any sort of way
But you will listen to me like the kids will too
Or else a man must do what a man must do

THAT BROTHER
Raised his voice and spoke down to me
Treated me like the child…
The woman he refused to see
He said that he owned me
That I would do as he said
And if I did not
He would go upside my head
Well,
I took it as word and walked away
Did as I was doing without hesitation
He asked, "Did you hear what I say?"
I said "Nigga please!"
And I meant it just like I said
"Let me get some stuff in your head…

I aint your tramp
I am not your piece or whore
If you want to trample me
You can take it out the door
I did not marry you to be mistreated
I did not need one to put me down
And if you think that this is what you will do
The wrong woman you have found
Now let me tell you before you speak
I respect every part of you as man
You may raise your voice and a few other things
But do not ever raise your hand…
To strike because I am a black woman
And I have been raised to be strong
You can put your hands several places on me
With my permission but upside my head it does not belong
Hear me now Baby…
I love you to death
And for you I would even choose to die
If it were necessary but please understand
That "beat down disposition" do not try"
I thought we were cool
I thought we had an understanding
He cooled out well
I thought we had found a landing
We were doing our thing
We were making tracks
Then he got tangled up with some others
And he had a setback
He walked in the door
And got in my total space
He raised his voice then his hand
And struck me in my face
It felt like fire
I sounded like thunder
I looked at him angrily
And I said, ": I do wonder…
If you forgot what I told you
In the very beginning?

I wonder if you recognize
I am not grinning?
I wonder if you think…
If you think I am standing hear
To submit to this degradation?
Do you think this is fear?"
He reached back once more
And I reached for my purse
Offering him a bullet and funeral
Plus, a ride in a hearse"
He cowered down
He apologized
I spoke to him "too late
You need to rise"
My finger trembled
I had not settled in my mind
Whether to shoot or save him
The Negro was in a real bind
He said "You will not kill me
You do not have the balls…"
I said "You will not be able to use yours
So now you make the call
Get on your knees
Say a real prayer
Trip if you want to
I offer you this dare
You see I am tired of you threatening me
I am tired of your trips with power
I am tired of having to look over my shoulder
Now you can meet your maker this very hour"
I put that pistol in his ear
I said "If you ever try this again
I promise to run through this bullet so true
That you will understand that although you are my man
You will not do what you want to do"
He said…" I believe…"
I said, "Shut up"
I prayed with eyes open
I had to be tough

But I did not mind going to jail
He hit me in my face hard and fast
I wanted the satisfaction of just
Kicking his a _ _
Just one time
But I felt sorry for him
I loved him and I felt the anger dim
I sat on the floor and said "Baby please
Do not stand up but get on your knees"
He felt me weaken…I did too
He felt this was his chance to do
What he needed to get through
He came to my waist…" Hell no Boo!"
I thought for a moment
Then picked up the phone
I said "Pick your poison Baby
It is jail or be gone"
I said "dial the number
Yes dial 9-1-1
You are going to like this
And for me this will be fun"
He slowly dialed like he was not sure
But he knew my patience would not long endure
He said hello when the operator came on the line
I said now you will do what I say this time
OR ELSE…
I said "repeat these words in her ear
Operator I call and I do fear
That I hit my wife and made a big mistake
I need help so that in the morning I may
On this side of a beautiful grassy ground
Trace this call and here my sorry butt may be found
I abused my wife like I had no sense
When she told me that such behavior would cross her fence
Have they left yet operator? This is serious
You must stay on the line while I discuss
My trifling behavior and stupidity
Operator are you still listening to me?
This is not the first time but it will be the last

Operator please hurry them I can feel the blast
Of gunpowder and shell in my head
I can see smoke and blood
I can taste the bitter lead
She is looking crazy by I dare not say
Anything that would take her in a detrimental way
Operator...she said thank you
For sparing my life
She will end this call
And cease being my wife
There is a knock at the door
She said I must go
Oh operator...
I love you so~"
The officer said "Mam please drop the gun"
I said I will after I am done
This man hit me with an open hand
And if after this he is released please understand
That if he ever comes back to this door
You can pick up next time bleeding on this floor
This is not a threat but a sincere pledge to do
What the system may be hesitant to do
I will not run scared nor be afraid of jail
No man will ever raise his hand to assail
Me and think that I will take it again
It is alright officers if you say AMEN!
I dropped the gun then said "I have had enough
Officer I will place my own self in cuffs
You must do your job so I will not fight
Arrest me and then read me my rights"
The officers looked at me and said you are
So much in control why don't you drive our car?
Take him in yourself and we will come along
Stupid he is and locked up is where he belongs
My husband said "Wait...you are giving her permission
To take charge of me?
They said it is called submission!

TALK ABOUT IT:

What I Read

What I Reflect on

What I Realize

How I Choose to Respond

How I can NOW reach out

THE SUICIDE OF WE

I come today to bid farewell
To say goodbye
To glance one last time at a loved one
Someone I have known all my life
I come to speak of his goodness
And mine
For I am he
Utilizing pronouns interchangeably
Although he was terribly flawed
Held a certain distinctiveness
He was unique in his own way
I address you and though we be few
A perfect trinity
I know you loved him as much as I
This man stood tall
Often cut back but never out
He changed circumstances
He was a transformer
He was a doer who often was done in
Because of those who he always did for
He spoke aloud
But who he had come to be known as
Was not who he was
And the myth survived the truth
The identity of a good man died
It fell into oblivion and never resurfaced
After screaming for recognition'
To a people who could care less
No one saw the sadness
The brooding
The aloneness
The fear and anxiety
Of trying to live in this world
Uncertain

As if my world is okay
Pressed down
Springing back fracturing himself
He tried to maintain
What he had not maintained
He became embitter
He became more than he was
Such a pretty baby they said
Such a handsome young man
Such a promising adolescent
Such a catch for some woman
Who were they speaking of?
Me?
Come on!
Him…
He was I and I am he
Lest you should become confused
So, this becomes a eulogy of 2 who are one
And then another
One half way whole
Another ill
And another dead yet drug around
Multidimensional
Living together yet never recognized
For the myriad and mess, we/I am
Can you hear me now?
I am silence
Like a soft voice in a crowded room
He became adjusted to it
Then he became it
Crushing his dreams
Negating his own identity
Smearing clarity with speculation
Turning inward where no voice is heard
But that of three who in such perfect agreement
That when they are wrong it is perfectly
And devastatingly so
He lived something
He tried

Age came
Diagnosis
Psychologists
Drugs and clinics
I told them
They told me
What?
Am I not smart enough to know me
With a 4.0 GPA at school
Legally doped
Living the high life
And you tell me to get ready for the world
Eighteen years of confusion
Drowning and reaching up
With a hand never taken
What do I have to look forward to?
At risk
A country divided
A backward walk into a captive situation
A crazy expectation
Begging rather than being blesses
Shot for walking
Shot for being black
Shot for being male
Shot for surrendering
And told it is my fault I was shot
And you say LOOK FORWARD TO THIS?
Am I what?
READY!
For the world…?
I am not ready for the house
Ready?
NOT READY~!
That was the cry and
Not for adulthood
Not for jobs
Not for the pressure of decisions
NOT READY
Not for responsibility

Not for relationships
That demanded of him
Not for identity
Seeking the self that maybe is lost
Among the authenticities in him
Not ready for jealousies
Critics and all the hell
They never tell you life holds
He did not ask for help
No more intrusions
Deeper inward became the plunge
Looking in his eyes all the while
Lost...where did he go?
Asking yet never answering my own self
This hole got deeper and more desirable
Withdrawal
Where is the pistol?
Give something
I need to calm these ...I think
But no~
I need a way out
I came without choice
I leave without conscience
Burying this stuff behind
I walk the path of the hidden
For those who know me best
Know me least and those who notice me
Still do not see me as I am so...
I shall say "bully be damn"
And take away your threats
You can kiss ...well, my behind
And another one like me find
Get it all
May the good people who watched you
Get a taste of your treachery
May the ones who gave no help
Did not understand
Refused to tell and speak
Above a mere whisper...

May you be found in isolation
For he and I was a good man
Insults and depression
I tire of feeling bad
And I do not want to talk
I do not want to fight
I do not want your help
I do not want your insight
I do not want company
I do not want anything
But PEACE
I want peace
I want to suck this barrel like a lollipop
And the kiss it eve so sweetly
Before squeezing a trigger and releasing euphoria
I have coveted so long and a sleep
No one can awaken me from
Quit trying to help me
I am fine
And so…
I come today to share
To speak of myself in multiple persons
To give to this world nothing
I come with humility for some
And the middle finger for others
Do not bury me for I do not want to be in this earth
Cremate me
Spare the expense
Let me hear no weeping at my departure
Nor rejoicing
Bury me at sea
Let me run in the ocean
Stand as you will and you will see a great man
Blow his brains all over this room
Because he wants to
And I do not have to see it
I come to say farewell
To me
I am in control

No man will be shooting me
No one else will control me
Including those who have
The rest of you are dismissed
The two of you remain
Turn off the sound
Kill the video
Close the door behind you
WE
Shall be done in a moment
Party over
Suicide?
I call it fond goodbye

TALK ABOUT IT:

What I Read

What I Reflect on

What I Realize

How I Choose to Respond

How I can NOW reach out

Do not be in such a hurry to grow up because after
you do you will forever be going up are not
permitted to return to these years ever again ~

Doris Lloyd

SLOW DOWN SON

Slow down
What are you looking for?
There is nothing out there but a hard way
It looks like fun
But what seems like freedom in nothing but a trap
Smell the scent but you will be denied
Slow down son, please slow down

Big man thinking outside the lines
He can get bigger if prey like you he finds
You want to fit in but you are a misfit
Stepping where you are going puts you in a pit
And they are eyeing you because you don't know
What things are nor where things go
You are unstable where you are and will be found
In a bad place ~ Son please slow down

You've been irritable and hard headed lately
You are acting like the street is your family
I smell the liquor and I smell the weed
Someone is planting in you a very bad seed
And you walk in here thinking it is okay
You thing that I really have nothing to say
But if you listen you will see and hear the sound
Of me crying slow down Baby, Son please slow down

She dresses cute but rather scanty
I see you taken by her panties
But where is she from and what does she do
To take such strong possession of you?
Slow down son and take possession
Of your own self ~ Shun the aggression
What the hell are you doing with a gun?
Slow down Baby, Slow down Son

Pocket full of money with no employment?
Crime is the pole to which you are bent
Expensive clothes and things unpaid for
Do not bring any more of it through my door
There is a bullet waiting for you for sure
Not long in this world shall you endure
Gangster and street life have left many on the ground
Slow down Son, please do slow down

You are full of good things but you want to be bad
You want what you think you should have had
You want to do protest and fight but not to be
You want to be what you were not raised to be
And let me tell you that YOU WERE RAISED
And in this foolishness, you shall not be praised
You shall not be a consideration nor understood
If you bring no value to the neighborhood

Do not get me wrong...I am Mama not your friend
I am where you started; I am where you begin
I gave you half of what you say you are and worth with
You added on to yourself Boy! You can cease with the fit
You can do what you want and act the fool
But the stuff in and of you is of my gene pool
If crash and wreck what you have it shall be found
You were living under the influence of stupidity refusing to slow down

Say What?
You do not want to hear what I must say?
Pack your stuff then and get out the way
In my house, you will not rant, rave and holler
You will not disrespect me and live on my dollar
You aint got a pot to piss in nor window to throw it out
You think that you have street credit and street clout
Step on and step into the place where many are found
Dead and victims because they would not slow down

I love you but I cannot watch what you are becoming

You shall be ever locked up or ever running
You will find no real contentment outside of the good
You cannot corrupt yourself and be good for the neighborhood
So, choose this day what you are going to do
I am giving you this advice and then Son that is good and sound
If you want to live long and good Son, you need to slow down

TALK ABOUT IT:

What I Read

What I Reflect on

What I Realize

How I Choose to Respond

How I can NOW reach out

OUTCRY

SO, Lord,
It is me
They called me
Said there had been an accident
I thought...Car? Fall? Something...else
But it was gunfire
A shooting
My child was shot
By strangers
Accident?
No!
I dressed to go to him
But no use
Reason? Yes!
Use...no!
Lifeless he lay
Helpless I stood
I just left the hospital
Yes, the one I brought him in the world in
He is dead
I felt his cold body
I saw him close his eyes
He tried to say goodbye
But those bullets got him
They took his life
They were not his
They had no business in him or on him
They belong in clips
Not bodies
I do not get it
And I am so mad!
Right now, I want to kill someone
These tears are not weak nor cold
They are filled with fervor and revenge

Do not ask me to act civil or think like you
Do not make me want to bust YOU in the face
I want to make someone feel what I do
I want to put my foot deep in his killer's ….
I really want to do something
WHY?
I took him to church
Dedicated him
Got him baptized
Took him to Sunday school
I raised him right
He was a good son
He got good grades
He was respectful
Why him?
You could have protected him
Why him?
Why all these piss poor
Low pants riding
Trifling
Thug wanna be but aint
Drinking drugging
Hanging out with no agenda
Violent in need of extermination
Artificial fellas out here…
Why mine?
WHY?
He was innocent
21 bullets!
Like a target on a range
Killed worse than a rabid dog
Was someone seeking a tear?
Is that what it was?
Was someone seeking to make a statement?
And what?
What now Lord?
He was coming home from church
Did he leave too early?
Why?

The steps of a good man are ordered by the Lord?
Did he mis-step?
O just want to know because … I just…
CAN YOU SAY SOMETHING?
I am listening with tears and snot
And I am not ashamed…
PLEASE ANSWER ME!
Do not be silent!
His blood is intermingling with the puddles of the morning
Rain that fell that did not flow has been colored
By the blood of my child
Your too young son gone
At the hands of a new breed of Cain
Eve had better resolve than me
And the police said…
It was just another random shooting
He was just another kid that will not count
He laid in the street riddled and did you see them
Looking aghast but what shall happen?
He shall fade like a vapor until the next comes
He shall not be remembered
I shall receive pity and cards but will there be justice?
No! I want no prison
Give me a gin, 21 bullets and the one who shot mine
Let me gun him down like the dog he is
LORD!!!!!!!!
I know I am out of line and control
But I cannot help it
21 years old and on his way
I am hurting!
My Baby is dead
And I must say goodbye
I must pretend not to know before a crowd
I must look down and say "I am Sorry"
I could not protect him
I am left with memories
Pictures and memories
What the hell…
If another person tells me to be strong…

FOR WHAT?
Shut up?
Rude? Yes! But necessary
You do not know my pain
Have you lost a child like this?
Answer!
How many have I angered now?
I am sorry...
I am just hurting
I am not angry but mad
I admit
If I could kill them all I would
But when this rage leaves
I will not exist as a victim
I shall not be a mourning mother without an agenda
I will not live in a noise without message
My passion will not permit my silence
I may close his casket
But never shall I close his case
Until what is taken is replaced
With SOMETHING
No one should feel this
I am tired of crying though I must cry
I will not be silent when these tears cease
I will not let my child die in vain
No!
I will not live "safely" in my house
While another child falls in the street
I WILL NOT!
I will not die because he was killed
But he shall live because I do
And he remains with me
I shall bleed and yet rise
From the bleeding place
And give life where there has been death
It is not over
He came forth of my blood
He left his blood here
It is not shed in vain

When a mother bleeds
When she touched by that of her child
Life comes is conceived
She becomes accommodating
Of something greater than what began
Hidden but ever growing
She shall bring it forth
And it shall rise
Though my baby be fallen
He is not through

TALK ABOUT IT:

What I Read

What I Reflect on

What I Realize

How I Choose to Respond

How I can NOW reach out

THE CASE

Why am I here today?
Why am I sitting in court?
Why am I on trial for harming a minor?
Why am I in orange attire and cuffs?
Why?
Because day before yesterday I said "No"
I had enough...
I love my child but I could go no further
He walked in MY house like it was his
He came in late and I was sleep
He wanted something to eat but I put up the food
His phone had been damaged
He had been smoking and drinking
At 17 years, old
I have tried to be understanding
He lost his dad 3 years ago
Killed by his mistress
For fooling around on her
With another woman and then beating her
I gave him a dad like that
Why?
How?
The sex was good
And the timing was wrong
My son is good but something went wrong
And I have let it run too long
Guilt plagued me and I let it get out of control
School problems though smart
Tied up in gang activity
Always the Teflon one
I called him my little man
The man of the house
Authority over his brother and sister
He vented

He took it
He started smelling himself
And I let him breathe deep too long
He assumed things and I tried to understand
Then he started acting like his daddy
It was like he rose from the dead
And I put up with it
Because I still had that sick tolerance
For the same old foolishness
And he was my baby
So, he acted just like him
Abusive and without regard for me
I took it
He got bigger and stronger
His scent grew and his breaths also
He got a little street credit
And thought it spent at home
Disrespect was his response to siblings
I taught them to be patient with him
To tolerate without agreeing
I lost control of my home
He took over until I woke up one day
This child addressed me as "BITCH"
And I decided that on that day I would bite
No more cursing
No more disrespect
No more ignoring
No more threatening
No more raising his voice at me
No more blatant disregard
No more…
Then he raised his hand to hit me
And the lights went out
Not in the house but in him
I hit him with a baseball bat
A plastic one but a bat nevertheless
I was tired and I told him while I beat him
No need to raise an eyebrow when I say beat
You do not spank a near grown man

I beat him…
I beat him with that bat until he was blue
I beat him with a wet bath towel until he was black
I beat him with my fists until I was satisfied
This was not discipline
I meant to hurt him
I meant to cripple that corruptness in him
I released every pinned-up response to his actions
I would not die at the hands of my child
And have my other children have to see it
I beat him YES I did
Because when a child rises against his mother
That child does not want a mother response
When he threatens to take life from one who gave it
TO HIM…
That is the end of the road
I called 911 and sat with him in my arms on the porch
I told them to send an ambulance for him
And the police for me
I knew I would go to jail
While we waited, I confessed my love
But I told him that if he ever raised his hand again
His total ass was mine and everything else
I re-instilled the fear of God in him
And I treated him as was needed
This was not the time for pity
And although he was scarred and wounded
I felt no remorse or regret for what I had done
He threatened to kill me
They would have called the medical examiner and funeral home
I called the police and paramedics…
When they arrived, I gave him to the paramedics
My son said "thank you"
He was glad to see someone other than me
His 6'2 length and 225 ponds seemed feeble
I walked away with no sense of remorse
I prayed and I went to the police officer humbly
"I said, Mr. Officer I did it
I whooped, disciplined and beat my son tonight

He was trying to kill me
But I refused to die
I refused to die in my spirit
I refused to die as a person
I refused to die as a mother
I refused to let him corrupt anymore
And have you have put a bullet in him
In the street and come to me to tell it
I refused to be disrespected and disregarded
I remembered he was heaven's gift to me
So tonight, I beat the Hell out of him
I cannot and will not die at the hands of my child
They said I should have called you first
But this was not about public law and order
This was about family loyalty and honor
What you could have done would have moved him
He would have gone to another place for a while
But it would not change him…the residue would remain
Of a child who has lost his way and almost his mind
This has gone on for a while and today I got tired
I had my pistol nearby and thought to shoot him
It is right over there in the third drawer from the bottom
Read me my rights
Never mind…I will do it myself
I have the right to remain silent…but I will not
Anything you say can and will be used against you…
I will be testifying
In a court of law…
Yada, yada, yada…
I am ready…let's ride
DO what you must do"
So, he did…
I came to jail and got dressed
I go to court today
I will not sugar coat what I have done
I am not angry anymore
I love my child
But I refuse to be a victim of his foolishness
I refuse to be bullied

I refuse to be afraid to direct and discipline
I refuse to let him think it is safe to disrespect me
He does not have to love me
That I MUST do
But he WILL respect me when he is around me
And when he walks in that door he will see MAMA
Or he will turn his high yellow tail around
Before the memories of the night I dealt with him return
And he experiences and encore performance of it
I will tell the judge…
"Your Honor
If you do not mind for a moment
I would like to demonstrate a thing or too
You see…I did not vote for you
But you are the judge
I respect that
When you walked in this place
We were all told to rise
We could lose our place in here if we did not
It would be seen as an act of contempt
EVEN if we did not vote for you or like you
Your honor I did not vote for you
And I do not know if I like you
But I respect you because of where you sit
If I disrespect you or are unruly
I am cited for contempt
Handled by the police
And removed from the premises
Well, that is what happened in my house
With my son
He came in wrong
He disrespected my honor
I charged him with contempt
I called the police to remove him
He will not disregard of disrespect me
In my own soul or home
You see, his daddy did this stuff
He saw him
And maybe he thought that gave him the right

To treat me like he does
But no!
No more bruises
No more bloodshed
No more being afraid to sleep
No more feeling guilty
No more making him feel justified
And empowered to do this to another woman
If you choose to lock me up again I am fine
Because I want you to know this
If my son comes back with me
I WILL SET THE RULES!
I never abused him but if he ever raises his hand
Against me or any other woman
In Jesus Name, I will bring him down
I will not let another have to kill what I birthed
I do not need a Family Service specialist to monitor me
This is what I will do with or without one
I have nothing to hide
Thank you for your kindness and patience"
I am cool with where I am today
I look forward to seeing my child
Emphasis CHILD!"

That is why I sit here
That is why I tell my story
I proudly own what I did
Could I have done something else?
YES! But this works for me
If they find me guilty I will gladly serve
If not, I will be the best mother possible
I will love my children
But I will raise them
I will bleed for them
BUT NEVER
Because of them
I will give my life for them
But never let them take it away
I am a Mother...

TALK ABOUT IT:

What I Read

What I Reflect on

What I Realize

How I Choose to Respond

How I can NOW reach out

The perpetuation of injustice without moral reprisal must not only be mourned and cited it must be dealt with for exposure and eradication from the highest to the lowest levels ~ Vern

BEFORE ANOTHER
TEAR IS CRIED

Repeatedly we come here
To speak a eulogy and a tear
To say I am sorry and walk away
To hug each other and to pray
We speak of change and then
Allow the same things to happen again
A soul, a group a community dies
The with tears we fill our eyes

But why? Why the same old thing
We have allowed this sorrow to sing
We have said OKAY let this be
And relive a different for of the same tragedy
Does it not make you mad...? Perhaps anger is better
America the beautiful allows its own stormy weather
Soldiers killed upon the base
College students killed in the learning place

Babies destroyed in broad daylight
A vigilante acquitted of guilt in what was not right
The killing of a man illegally selling cigarettes
What did a multi-people force have to fret?
Senseless murder in Missouri we deplored
Then let it happen again in Baltimore
We terrorize our own people every day
They think others want to hear what we must say

The racism of the 20th century was not killed but put away
It has borne new generations that thrive to this day
They have taken off hoods and now wear suits and ties
The persona is the same despite the disguise

It hurts us all and is breeding even more
Destruction and disunity hangs at our door
We yield the truth, justice and right
We have allowed old ghosts to referee the fight

21st century president with blood black and white
After newness, has worn off is not received right
Is not acknowledged as a living metaphor
Of the dream that America has asked for
Violence against the White House other labeling
Have endangered him and those to the table he brings
What is the verdict of a people who make up the court
Of public opinion? Continue or abort?

What is stirring?
What shall be said?
Who shall judge?
How shall this be led?
It is all of us
We are all ears
But this environment continuously
Feeds our frustrations and fears

Not Guilty
Insane
Well there is not enough
To convict the perpetrator and it is tough
Is the frequent verdict that is written
To a country venomously infected and bitten
By the snakes we permit to slither along
Now some of you may think I am wrong

For writing like this on this particular day
But hear these words I must say
Because I know what it is like in this land
To be mistrusted for being black, strong and Man
A white man is seen often as less than he can be
If he yet walks and works strongly with me
I have a place in my country but it is with ceiling

Let me break through it and the system will be squealing

My sisters are obviously black but many are too
Red, yellow, brown and of many different hues
Every person does not have the same faith as me
But WE are the family of US ~ ONE HUMANITY
We are restricted if we stay in place
Never crossing the lines that put on us a new face
I am tired of this and it needs to be said
Another kind of thinking must come to our heads

Land of the free and home of the brave
We stand in allegiance while our flag is waved
Yet we repeat this over and over again
It is certainly time that we begin
To see that it is not only others who gun us down
We have permitted injustice to hang around
It can be seen clearly with no explanation
It is deeply embedded even in this generation

Black lives matter and all others do too
But tell me NOW what shall we do?
Not another can afford to be wasted
Until real change can truly be tasted
HEAR ME AMERICA! This is epidemic
This is our fight...WE ARE IN IT
If others did this, we would do more than discuss
What happened and they would have to deal with us

I hear hearse wheels' roll
I hear mournful cries
Rightfully so for those slain
It is needed to say goodbye
To those slain by an evil hand
Tomorrow where will this nation stand?
Security will not protect us from what is so deep in
The fabric of our nation ~ an acceptable sin

So, no more condolences and allow this to continue

Do what is necessary for a nation to do

One nation indivisible with liberty and justice for all
Shall be a declaration discredited and soon fall
In the eyes of many who watch us as we stand
Appearing unified in word but hot heart and hand
It is a matter of purpose, dignity and pride
We must make changes before another tear is cried

TALK ABOUT IT:

What I Read

What I Reflect on

What I Realize

How I Choose to Respond

How I can NOW reach out

Female is the gender of a woman and what she is given to work with. Distinction is the stamp that she puts upon it that renders her beyond ordinary ~ Vern

WOMAN OF DISTINCTION

...And God said "let there be" until the sixth day
Then He decided to do things a different way
From red clay and gifts from of Euphrates and Nile
By his hand, He formed His first child

He called him Adam ~ the very first man
He created one more by his hand
Who would be Adam's blessed unsolvable mystery
And be an inseparable part of his history

Taken from and formed out of his rib-bone
I am God's solution to man's problem of "alone"
So beautiful and magnificent that even angels recognized
Along with man, that I am God's most precious prize

To him I am wife, friend and lover
I am his helpmeet; he is my cover
I am his garden ~ his alone
He is my gardener ~I the garden his seed will be sown

I am the queen and giver of birth
To every good and special thing in the earth
In me God works so very specially
Those things that happen when He says "Let there be"

I am strong, sensitive, kind and resilient
I am beautiful, passionate, desirable and intelligent
I am a visionary with a keen sense of sight
I am an achiever who knows how to exercise might

I am a starter and finisher of whatever I choose to do
I refuse to give up until the task is through
I am compassionate, brave and very bold
I am sensitive in body, spirit and soul

I am so capable that you cannot doubt me
I am so necessary that you cannot live without me
I am so lovely that the mind cannot conceive
How God could bring forth so much out of Eve

I AM A WOMAN OF DISTINCTION

TALK ABOUT IT:

What I Read

What I Reflect on

What I Realize

How I Choose to Respond

How I can NOW reach out

Where the seed is weak the plant shall be also. Be mindful of what you plant knowing that it shall only bring forth what it is ~ Vern

THE STRONG BLACK MAN

Brothers from all dimensions let me share some knowledge
That many have not learned in school and college
I am not disregarding what you learned at the university
But there are some insights that need to be from me
I AM THE STRONG BLACK MAN
What does that mean?
I AM Strong
I AM Black
I AM a Man

Do not judge by what you think you see
I am more than the present
I am the product of my history
I am discoverable and learnable, not a mystery

I am honorable, royal dignifiedly human
I AM THE STRONG BLACK MAN
Let me tell of my lineage, of my descent
I am of the soil of the Dark Continent
Nursed at the breasts of Euphrates and Nile
Kidnapped and transported across the miles

Stripped from my mother's arms and native name
Ripped from royal robes I was crowned with shame
Threats, drownings, beatings and exits from lofty cliffs
 Considered more than animals, human but only three fifths

Given, sold, bought, scattered over a foreign land
Raised not as a child but a lowly field hand
Instructed that an education for me was not needed
My lot in life was fulfilled if a cotton field was seeded
Beaten till bloody if I held and pursued another position
You see for my children I knew there would be a transition
I refused to accept them bowing, never being able to Stand

So, I took what they gave…
I AM THE STRONG BLACK MAN

I have written and sang the songs that got us through
I have sacrificed by doing the things that I had to do
I have worked without pay, I have held many doors
That I could only stand at while others covered the floor
But I learned what was available and determined to give
To my children the same opportunity to freely live
Not as a servant to those who controlled the door
Taking only what was left after all had left the floor
I am the King of beautiful intelligent African Queen
Even though often denied her love and chased off the scene
She carried my seed and never denied me true honor
She bore the burdens and challenges that were put upon her
She birthed and she nursed our children and others
She was the epitome of the genuine mother
She was my spine; she was the bone in our back
She kept our family and our people on track
She was the lowly slave yet the desire of the master
There was no other woman that he pursued faster
And though raped and mistreated she held it together
It was about more than NOW…it was about being better
She was the Eve that held this Adam's Hand
And helps me proudly declare…
I AM THE STRONG BLACK MAN

Now look at me you who stand on the other side
Of slavery, oppression, segregation and apartheid
You are the generation that must certainly lift
Yourselves above the standards set for you and use the gifts
That was given to you to establish your stand
In this age as…
THE STRONG BLACK MAN

I give you my eyes to see beyond where you presently are
To cast vision that begins where you stand but goes afar
I give you ears to hear life's sweetest songs
The mouth to sing them when right or when wronged

I give you a mind to think rather than to react
To create when there is little and you suffer lack
Arms to lift the burdens and challenges you will surely face
Shoulders to carry your children from place to place
Hands to shape and then to willingly extend
To others as brothers, comrades and friends
Legs to stand before kings in pride and with dignity
Feet to leave prints for the next generation to see
That though you have advanced there is more to do
They must learn the same lessons that I have taught you

Pull your pants up
Hold your head up
Straighten your back up
Lift your eyes up
Hold your woman up
Lift your children up
Hold your people up
Lift your GOD up
Lift your voice up
Let it be heard throughout the land
You are my hope a dream
You are the Legacy
OF THE STRONG BLACK MAN

TALK ABOUT IT:

What I Read

What I Reflect on

What I Realize

How I Choose to Respond

How I can NOW reach out

WISDOM TO A SON

Young Man… let God make you what you would be before getting involved with anyone else. Who you will become must be start with the one who made you. Learn in his presence. Inquire of him regarding your nature, your makeup, your drives and destiny. Learn what matters most. Let your spirit connect with the great God of the universe. Learn his ways and directives. Ask him how to handle your situations so that your situations do not handle you. Become a learner, an industrious man, a creative and expressive man who values what God has given him in his own self. Learn what it is to love and how to receive love. Love him and you will discover what real life feels like. You will need it as you go.

Young Man… learn to love yourself. Do not put yourself in last place or any other subordinate position. Do not love yourself because of where you come from because value is not found on the fringes but in the depths. Do not despise where you come from or who you emerge from. You may receive a critique by someone that declares that your mama is no good or that your father is not worth a quarter but remember that all that you are composed of comes from those two individuals. You are the miraculous result of a powerful engagement of sperm and ovum. You have been a conqueror from the beginning for your very birth was a nine-month journey coming forth from nothing to someone who would grow and present his self on the world stage ready to make a difference. Love your mind and treat it as if you do. Feed your heart and let the best of affection be its composition. Let no one teach you that coldness is powerful and what men do to guard it. Open it again and again and reach out to others with it. DO not fear it being hurt. If you fill it with love it can never be destroyed and can recover from any situation it encounters. Lift with your hands and dream great dreams. See a thing from God's perspective and that includes you. You will appreciate things much more.

Young Man when you look for a woman do not seek her in the wild. Do not seek someone that you would not give your life for. Do not seek a woman who must demean herself to lift you up. Do not seek a woman of uncontrolled passions and undisciplined behaviors. Seek a woman who walks with God and yet is uniquely her own woman. Seek a woman that you can cover and be exclusive to. You do not need a woman who has only a desire for you but no need of you. Seek a woman that God will show you and one whom he releases into your life with instructions on how to handle her. Love her out of your person, your presence, your power and your passion. Cleave to her and let her see and feel how much you love God and yourself. Feed her out of the two loves that you have mentioned to her fullest capacity...talk about influence.

Young Man love your children. They are of your loins. Love them actively and they will never be neglected. They will need you to talk to, to play with, to teach and to model the behaviors that you will display to them. TAKE TIME TO LOVE THEM FOR REAL. They need your discipline and direction. Love them when they are right and when they are wrong. Love them when all in you says they are not worth it because that voice that may speak that untruth is the same voice that compelled Adam to abandon the will of God. Your children will be learning what you have already been through and one day they will thank you for waiting on them. So many young people are unloved and devoid of fatherly love. Be the blueprint of the type of man your sons will want to be and your daughters will desire to have. They may choose different details but give them the right design. Love the mother who birthed them and permitted you to enter her sanctuary and participate in the precious conception of
your children

Young Man love others. You cannot build a life with bitterness and isolations. You cannot be a solo warrior. You cannot use the world and not love it. You cannot be the "only one." You cannot look for women to be like you and judge other men based on your personal standard. You give to others what God has given to you and what you give to yourself. You must run from the assumptions that tears reveal weakness and big boys don't cry. You must not leave sensitivity in the hands of a woman alone. You must not accept the destructive encouragement to sow your wild oats and disrupt the lives of a woman through illicit behavior. The love you share will season the world you live in.

Young Man feed your soul with excellence. Feed it with excellent entertainment, excellent music, excellent recreation and excellent family moments. A fish who lives in tainted water can never appreciate good water even if it is better. Do not simply become accustomed to the environment that may be prevalent at the time but have a desire for higher things. Read good books. Listen to music that soothes and motivates the soul. Embrace your culture and celebrate your natural surroundings. Take time to create moments that have their greatest cost from what you invest from your spirit.

Young Man take care of yourself physically. You will need your body as you go along. It is what you use to contact others. It makes you visible and permits you to participate in the affairs of the world. Remember that quality of life is as important as quantity of life. Your body is a temple of the Holy Spirit Therefore God ought to be glorified in it. You will find your esteem will increase and your children and grandchildren can participate in some of your strength. Your woman can enjoy the eye candy that she should not always have to look for outside of home and can still have an able lover in the fall and winter of her life. Do not leave her a widow in the prime of her life because you choose to be neglectful. Take care of yourself young man

FOR...

Young Man you will become an old man. The best of what you have will enter decline and you will not live by your strength by your wisdom. You will model and mentor those who have what you used to have. You will not be sought after for your finance but for your footsteps. Young man you will become aware of your true mortality and even if you live to be one hundred you will understand that no matter how well the best of us live we ultimately die as will the worst of us. You cannot stop the inevitable but young man live in such a way that when you are laid to rest you leave more than a memory to be clung to for a moment. Leave a legacy that can be built upon and continued. Leave your sons an agenda and investment that is enough for them to live on the interest while increasing the principal for generations to come. Do not merely seek to be a father but a patriarch in your family and community.

Young Man I share as a senior man who has been where you are. More years have been spent than are left but I approach the fall and winter of life with great anticipation that what I have given thus far has roots beyond my years. Let me give to you this wisdom. May you take it much further with your strength. Young Man I am proud to be a man like you.

TALK ABOUT IT:

What I Read

What I Reflect on

What I Realize

How I Choose to Respond

How I can NOW reach out

Bless a young woman in her budding, when what is desired is not evident, for what is desired of is not possible in her blooming without it ~ Vern

WISDOM TO A DAUGHTER

My Daughter I am a man and the first man who had an investment in you. In part, you exist because of the investment of me in you coupled with the investment of your mother. When I look at you I see me so when it may appear that I am a little over-protective please understand that I do not merely see a baby girl. I see MY baby girl. I see a beautiful creation in the image God. I see an amazing creation entrusted to me whom I am responsible to bless until there is one who will be willing to give to you what I give to you now. My daughter the best of live never emerges from the pocket but out of the person.

My Daughter let God define your womanhood. Take time to understand the uniqueness of who you are. Understand that as He created manhood so He created womanhood. Let him cultivate the special creation that you are. For you to assume your rightful place in this world it is important that you become who you are before you become engaged with any other person. Embrace your culture and identity. Expand your horizons. Be qualified to stand in the shoes of Esther or rule from the throne as Cleopatra, Sheba or Nefertiti. Stay close to Him because he can uncover for you mysteries that a man must discover with your permission. Stand up for who you were created to be and not what many have challenged you to accept.

My Daughter come to know who you are and embrace that. Celebrate your beauty. Look in the mirror and see not only what is on you but what is in you. Brighten your eyes, take care of your smile, tenderly treat your skill, strengthen your stand and build your arms. Treat your hair as a crown. Pamper yourself. Tell yourself how fine you really are. Make your jeans glad that you wore them because of how you walk. Teach your dresses and skirts what it is to have that confident swagger and naturally sexy sway.

Embrace your femininity without exploiting the mysteries of your womanhood. Do not put on common display that which is to be reserved for committed and covenant relationship. Let your make-up accentuate who you are without creating a "you" no one can recognize when you do not have it on. Do it because it is what God would have you to do and you need to become accustomed because that is what queens need.

My Daughter Cultivate your mind. Learn from the model of wise women who currently reign. Walk with your sisters as you are raised but understand that all learning comes from one who has come before you and helps to chart a course for you. Do not let the friendship of your friends cause you to lose the modeling of your mother. They will agree with you and assure you that what you feel is often correct. There is nothing wrong with that but she will help you to understand real womanhood. Not: be careful of subjecting yourself to the ultimate instruction of a person who is in the same class as you. Remember that there is a big difference between being the smartest person in the class and being the professor.

My Daughter do not leave your father to pursue your boyfriend. A man who would truly have you will come to your father and seek you. He understands that he is looking to assume that man role that your father has and it makes him face the ultimate man test. You will different boyfriends and it is unwise for you to entrust to one whom you will have known so little what it has taken your father the first of your lifetime to build. If two fathers cannot go with you in any relationship, then the relationship is not worthy of you. As the Father would not release Eve to Adam without condition so should you not look to break away from you heavenly
Father or paternal father without condition.

My Daughter marry only a man who wants you for you. If you must pursue him then he will continue to run from you. If he comes for you then he will continue to come for you. Show yourself a lady always and never look to be what you are not. You are a woman. You are a lady. You will need a man who desires to bless you and make you his priority. Listen to how he talks about his mother. Observe how he engages your parents. Before you say "I do" make sure that the man you desire is "made." and not just male composition. Just as a cake is merely flower, butter, milk and eggs in the raw you will need more than male, you will need man. If you have the choice between a man who will love you and one who will provide for you choose the one who will love you. Why? Because the man who will love you will always seek the best of provision for you but the man who only provides may never really choose to love you. You will be his wife. Make sure that he is one that you will want to give to and that you can trust with your offerings. Let him love you, lead you without controlling you, share with you, succeed and fail with you. Never put anything or anyone in front of your marriage and never leave him to his self. His best choices are made with you. His worst are made without you. Remember, it is not good for a man to be alone.

My Daughter when you have children remember to raise them as a mother. You are equipped with the heart to love them, the spirit to understand them, the breasts to nurse them, the hip to ride them and the words to communicate as no other person can. You are the ultimate field and giver. They will love you as they love no other person but always live on the plane of motherhood. You will give as no other can and they will reach to you as no one else. Be careful who you parent with. Your child will be fifty percent of who you are and fifty percent of who that other person is so make sure you choose wisely. Feed them what they need more than what they want. Do not fear their tear or cries but be prepared to comfort and dry them. Direct them delight in them and discipline them. Teach them as you have learned and do not be afraid to get help. Motherhood is an honor and they will honor you for being a good mother.

My Daughter I have tried to live in such a way that you could see the true man in me. I have tried to give you a model of what a man should be and how he should conduct his affairs. You have seen my strengths and my failings. You are privy to my emotions, my intellect, my passions and irritabilities. You know what I stand for and who I stand for. I have tried to honor your mother in a manner that lets you know that you should start no lower than that and I am here for you because no matter what you may have learned recently, I am the man that knows you and manhood better than anyone else. My daughter do not take that lightly and do not walk away from me because I am your father and much of what is in you is what has come from me. You are so much a part of me!

TALK ABOUT IT:

What I Read

What I Reflect on

What I Realize

How I Choose to Respond

How I can NOW reach out

A woman may become many things in the life to a child and despite, at times, our best efforts at detachment we find that she always seems to be connected to the most important parts at times of us. From apron strings to heart strings we remain connected ~ Vern

STRINGS ATTACHED

Thank God for all the gifts He gives
To mothers so richly that we might live
Eyes to watch; mouths to sing and speak
Breasts to nurse; arms to hold us when we are weak

Ears to hear; a back and hip to ride
Hands and legs that keep us by their sides
Feet to lead and hands for what we mishandle to catch
Thank God moms come with strings attached

The months preceding every child's birth
Are shared with only one person on earth
Who nurtures us until we are hatched
Thank God moms come with strings attached

After we are born and seek independence
We want mom to know we are in attendance
So, we run and play while she works and sings
Never far away from her apron strings

She is mommy, teacher, friend and guide
She comes from a special batch
Of God ordained people who with us abide
Thank God, she comes with strings attached

TALK ABOUT IT:

What I Read

What I Reflect on

What I Realize

How I Choose to Respond

How I can NOW reach out

For more information on Only Mothers Bleed or to have us come to

To stay updated on what we are doing visit us on Facebook at OnlyMothersBleed@strengthtosorrow

Look for the soon to be released DVD produced by Dr. Michelle Harris documenting the story of women who have bled and are helping others to overcome and bring new life into their personal lives and communities entitled Only Mothers Bleed.

63298219R00057

Made in the USA
Lexington, KY
03 May 2017